SO YOU'RE

60!

Mike Haskins & Clive Whichelow

Illustrations by Andy Hammond

summersdale

SO YOU'RE 60!

This edition copyright © Mike Haskins and Clive Whichelow, 2013
First published in 2007
Reprinted 2008, 2009, 2010, 2011

Illustrations by Andy Hammond

An Hachette UK Company
www.hachette.co.uk

Summersdale Publishers Ltd
Part of Octopus Publishing Group Limited
Carmelite House
50 Victoria Embankment
LONDON
EC4Y 0DZ
UK

www.summersdale.com

Printed and bound in Malta

ISBN: 978-1-84953-439-0

Substantial discounts on bulk quantities of Summersdale books are available to corporations, professional associations and other organisations. For details contact general enquiries: telephone: +44 (0) 1243 771107 or email: enquiries@summersdale.com.

To..............................

From...........................

INTRODUCTION

Well look at you! Congratulations! You are 60 years young! I said CONGRATULATIONS, DEAR! YOU'RE 60 YEARS YOUNG! YES! Idiots who talk to you like that are going to irritate the hell out of you from now on.

Yes, you're 60. But so what? Sixty's not old these days is it? You don't feel old, do you? You don't look old. OK, you don't look that old.

You're the same as ever. Nothing's changed. You're fit as a flea. A flea whose knees are giving him a bit of gyp maybe. But still basically fit. OK, there's that pain in your neck as well. And that funny thing you can feel round the back somewhere. But apart from that there's nothing much wrong. It's not as though you've gone gaga. So what if you can't immediately remember your children's names?

Sixty is a great age to be – in more ways than one! So let me just say in conclusion, you're marvellous for your age. I said I THINK YOU'RE MARVELLOUS FOR YOUR AGE, DEAR! YES!

Here's to the next 60 years!

THE BASIC MYTHS ABOUT TURNING 60

You'll be treated with respect everywhere you go – as long as you only go places where you'll meet other people the same age as you

You'll be able to enjoy a nice, long, well-earned rest – and that's just after walking up the stairs

THINGS YOU WILL NEVER NOW DO

Be the new face of Estée Lauder

Get the hang
of computers

YOUR LIFE WILL NOW CONSIST OF

*Sleeping during sex
instead of after it*

Being told to slow down by your GP rather than by the police

Having the Radio Times
*as your social calendar
for the week*

DRESS CODE FOR THE OVER 60S – SOME DOS & DON'TS

*Do remember –
almost anything goes
with grey*

*Don't try wearing a thong –
your flesh may resemble a
bunch of uncooked sausages
stuffed in a string bag*

Do wear the psychedelic dayglo fashions of your youth – not only will people see you coming, it'll be easier for you to find your clothes in the dark

Don't take fashion advice from anyone older than yourself

TIPS ON HOW TO APPEAR YOUNGER THAN YOU ACTUALLY ARE

Paint your neck so those skin-folds look like a trendy scarf

Try liposuction using an attachment on your vacuum cleaner

GIVEAWAYS THAT WILL TELL PEOPLE YOU ARE OVER 60

Turning the music down and the TV up

Reminiscing about when there was no swearing on TV

A GUIDE TO HOW OTHERS WILL NOW PERCEIVE YOU

Someone who will still be crossing when the green man starts flashing

The originator of all odd smells

THE MAIN EVENTS IN YOUR LIFE YOU CAN NOW LOOK FORWARD TO

The fashion trends of your youth becoming recognised as classics

Getting new hips – at long last you can be genuinely bionic!

THINGS YOU'LL FEEL SMUG ABOUT

Going to a funeral and coming home again afterwards

Having a no-claims bonus record that predates the birth of the person you deal with at the insurance company

Having all your own teeth

Having all your own hair

THE MAIN EVENTS IN YOUR LIFE THAT ARE LESS EASY TO LOOK FORWARD TO

Having your first chamber pot – for 'emergencies'

Getting breathless blowing out your birthday cake candles

Having people talk about you as though you're not actually there while popping toffees in your mouth whether you asked for them or not

CONVERSING WITH YOUNG PEOPLE

(PART 1)

What you say and
what they hear

*'Isn't my new grandson/
granddaughter lovely?' =
'I'm available for babysitting
24/7'*

'I was out at work by the time I was fourteen' = 'I was a Victorian child chimney sweep'

'I'm not feeling too well' =
'Congratulations! You are
about to come into your
inheritance!'

CONVERSING WITH YOUNG PEOPLE

(PART 2)

What they say and
what you hear

*'How do you prune a
rose bush?'* =
*'Can you come round and
prune my rose bush?'*

'Would you like to come over for dinner?' =
'There's a good takeaway nearby. Maybe you'd like to pay as well?'

'I've got you a special birthday present this year' = 'Have you got round to making your will yet?'

THINGS YOU CAN NOW GET AWAY WITH THAT YOU COULDN'T PREVIOUSLY

Making no effort whatsoever to lose weight

Acting like the grumpy old git you know you've always been

*Flirting outrageously
with members of the
opposite sex*

Saying exactly what you think

THINGS YOU WON'T BE DOING AGAIN

The lotus position

Seeing in the New Year and enjoying it

SHATTERING
MOMENTS SOON
TO COME

Your (or your partner's) semi-annual erection becomes an annual semi-erection

You bend down to see if you can still touch your toes and then forget what you went down there for

THINGS YOU SHOULD NOT HAVE IN YOUR HOME

Any of your children

An unlicensed firearm

AARGHH! THINGS YOU NEVER THOUGHT WOULD HAPPEN

You forget your
own birthday

The sound of a dripping tap causes you to become desperate to go to the toilet

YOUR NEW
OUTLOOK
ON LIFE

Your idea of multitasking is sleeping and not dribbling at the same time

Your idea of a white-knuckle ride is travelling on an escalator

*Your idea of a
dangerous sport
is tiddlywinks*

THINGS YOU WON'T BE DOING ON HOLIDAY ANY MORE

*Starting the day,
drinking session straight
after breakfast*

Midnight skinny-dipping

REASONS TO
BE CHEERFUL

*Your secrets are
safe with your friends
because now they can't
remember them*

*All those charities
you gave to – it's
payback time!*

If you're interested in finding out more about our books, find us on Facebook at Summersdale Publishers and follow us on Twitter at @Summersdale.

www.summersdale.com